THE ESCAPE

How I Ran from Shame to Fame

Oliver Nakakande

CONTENTS

DEDICATION

I dedicate this book to every young girl and woman who dares to dream. Your dream is valid. Work at it, and it shall come to pass.

ACKNOWLEDGEMENT

First, I thank Almighty God for life and for giving me the courage to share my story.

I acknowledge the young girls in Uganda who trust me enough to share their stories with me. I draw inspiration from their stories to raise awareness on the issues we face as young women.

Finally, I thank myself for the courage I have gained over the years, to share my story and inspire millions of girls around the world.

PREFACE

For your guidance!

Whatever you believe in becomes your conviction. Freedom and redemption lie only in conviction!

The Escape; How I Ran from Shame to Fame addresses only those who believe they deserve a better future regardless of whatever life throws at them. The truth is, people will throw stones at you, please don't throw them back; collect them and build an empire.

This book will strike only those who still carry a spark of truth, a pang of insatiable hunger for success, and a yearning to be actual human beings. To all such, it will become a shining light and staff and will unswervingly lead them out of the chaos of present-day confusion.

The Escape is intended as the torch to help all serious listeners or readers find the right path, which leads to the longed-for height. It is intended to lead them 'from being a problem to a solution to the problem'.

Only those who bestir themselves can succeed in life. The fool who uses extraneous aids for this, in form of the ready-made opinions of others, only walks his path as if on crutches while ignoring his healthy legs.

But, the moment he boldly uses the abilities that lie dormant within him and awaits his call for help, he begins to employ the talent entrusted to him and follows his Creator's Will to overcome all obstacles that seek to divert him.

Awake therefore! Genuine faith lies only in conviction, and conviction comes solely through an inflexible weighing and examining. See that you are indeed alive in the beautiful creation of your God!

Annet Iragaba Bakunzi

Private Secretary to His Excellency

The President of Uganda, on Legal affairs

WHY I WROTE THIS BOOK

I decided to share my story with the world because of two reasons. First, I feel it's the right time to tell my story and share what I went through in childhood and teenhood and how I came to be who I am today.

Second, I want people especially young girls to be inspired by my story and to understand that they can be anything they want to be if they work hard at it enough.

In sharing my story, I want to create awareness about sexual abuse issues that happen against young girls and how immediate and extended family members typically handle such issues. More often than not, these issues are covered up or swept under the carpet due to the shame and stigma involved.

However, by writing this book, I encourage teenage girls not to keep quiet. There's always a way out of such unpleasant situations, if they think deeply enough and run for help.

By sharing the plan I put in place and executed to escape sexual abuse, I show to teenage girls that they're never helpless and that they're stronger and more resilient than they give themselves credit for. This book equips them to be ready to take decisive steps if they ever find themselves in such situations.

With hindsight, I advise any teenage girl who finds herself in similar situations to report the abuser or tell someone she trusts about it. When it happened to me, it was hard to find someone to talk to, but many helplines are available to call nowadays. No teenage girl should be abused, and no abuser should go scotfree.

I understand that many girls face this situation at one time or the other and not many of them come out of it unscathed. But with this book, I want to raise awareness and give a voice to teenage girls in Uganda and all around the world. I want to inspire and teach them that no matter what they go through, they should remain focused and true to themselves.

CHAPTER 1
MY CHILDHOOD

As a little girl, my main goal and aspiration in life was to be rich and successful. I didn't know how it would happen, but I always knew that I was made for more than my immediate circumstances showed me. I come from a large but close-knit family and my earliest memories of childhood were of my aunts, uncles and cousins gathering in the garden of one of my uncles or aunts during the holidays or festive seasons to eat, drink, play and have a good time. I loved the Christmas celebrations most because almost everyone would be on holidays, and we always had lots to eat and drink. I was born in Kampala, the capital city of Uganda and being an urban center made things even more interesting because we had lots of fun places to visit during holidays. We were not rich, but we were a family that really loved being together. The times I had much more fun was before my parents separated. I made many friends from the neighborhood, and we used to have dinners together.

My dad usually took my siblings and I on travels around the country, and everything just seemed okay because he could afford these fun places and create memories with us. My nursery school was next door to our home at the time, and my mom used to pack my lunch and give me sweets and cakes to take to school. Everything was just so perfect, but those beautiful memories lasted until reality hit and my mom moved out of our home taking my sister and I with her. I know how much she struggled to bring us up and those times were some of the hardest times of my life.

As a child, it didn't matter that my parents were separated and each person had moved on with their lives, what mattered most to me was that we all came together from time to time as one big family and celebrated life, good health and good fortune. However, as I grew older and as much as I enjoyed being with my cousins during the holidays, I missed having a complete family.

My parents separated when I was about 9 years old. I clearly remember the fights they used to have and how I would run to my room and try to cover my ears with my clothes to shut out all the shouting and noise. At first, I didn't know why they were always quarreling but as I grew older, I understood that it was because of other women. My dad was polygamous in nature, and my mom couldn't stand it. She believed that a man is meant to get married to only one woman till death do them part and so even though my dad remarried after they separated, my mom did not. It wasn't until I became a teenager that I asked for details from my mom. At first, she didn't want to tell me or any of my siblings because she didn't want us to grow up to hate our father. But, I told her that I needed to know why my family was different from that of my friends in the neighborhood or at school. I had a large number of aunts, uncles and cousins who gathered regularly during family celebrations—naming ceremonies, birthdays, weddings—festivities and holidays, yet I longed for my own immediate family to be together. So, she explained what happened.

Some men have the mindset that they can have as many women as they want, but my mom wanted to be the only woman in his life and home. At a point, when she understood that she couldn't stop him from having relationships with other women, she made it clear that she didn't want another woman to live in the same house with us.

But after one of their many fights and in order to spite her, my dad brought another woman to live with us. That was the straw that broke the camel's back and caused their separation. She moved out with my elder sister and I and remained single. By the way, my mom and dad were not legally married; they were just a man and woman who had children together. So, it wasn't like they needed to be officially divorced after the marriage ended. Now, my dad is with someone else but they are also not legally married. They just live together, and they have children together. He has three other children from his other relationships. This means that from my parent's and my father's marriage, I have five siblings. One of them has passed away, so I have two sisters and two brothers now.

When I think about it now, I see that much more than the food, drink and play that my siblings and cousins enjoyed when we were together, I also inculcated certain values during that period of my life. The values of integrity, sincerity, creativity, discipline, innovativeness, foresight and commitment that I manifest today, were developed as I interacted with my immediate and extended family; as a child. These value systems helped to groom me and made me stand out everywhere I go. These values come into play as I interact with people all over the world and do what I can to make the world better for all of us. These values are my trademark so that when I have done my bit and my time is over, I would be remembered as an inspiration that helped girls and women find their voice, discover who they truly are and become the best versions of themselves.

But, was my life just a rollercoaster of parties and happy moments? What did I go through to become who I am today? What did I do to turn out better than my circumstances and experiences dictated for me? Why did I decide to write this book? Who do I desire to help by sharing my life story and experiences this way?

Come with me as I unveil the answers to these questions and more in subsequent chapters.

CHAPTER 2
AWAY ON HOLIDAYS

I grew up in Kawempe division in Kampala. I attended nursery and primary school and did three years of my high school there, before I moved away. I changed school in the fourth year of high school, when I went to live with my father's sister. Even though life with my mom and sister was somewhat hard, I didn't complain, because I was loved and allowed to be who I wanted to be in our home. Our routine was quite simple; in the mornings, my sister and I did our chores and afterwards prepared for school, while my mom prepared to go to her shop. She had a retail shop in a building not far from the main market where she sold household necessities. When we were done with school in the afternoon, we would go and meet her in the shop and help her sell until we closed in the evening. She also sometimes sold fruits and items that she knew people in the area might need. But, as I helped my mom to sell and make money, I knew I would do more than that when I grew up. I wanted to be famous and live a more comfortable life because of the things I saw around me.

Many times, whenever I was sent on errands, I had a pasttime. I would go to the Kawempe interstate motor parks and watch the travelers. I usually admired the pretty well dressed ladies seated in the cars and would deliberately walk beside the windows of the cars to have a good look at the dresses and shoes they wore. I also loved to catch a whiff of their perfumes. Looking at those women fueled my desire to do better with my life and look like one of them when I grew up. As I watched the travelers, I learned that there is a life much better than the one I was living and which I could aspire to and achieve if I worked hard enough.

"Heiii! What are you still doing here, I've been looking everywhere for you," my sister barked at me from behind an empty van waiting to be loaded; on one of such days.

I had been staring absentmindedly at a tall dark-skinned lady who had just bought a bottle of drink from a hawker and was asking for a straw to have her drink with. She wore a knee-length Ankara print dress and strappy sandals that matched the color of the dress. Her thick jet black hair was done up in a coiffure, and I noticed that she had no jewelry on. The dress had a low neckline that didn't show her cleavage but clung to her curvy stature in a classy way. I guessed she was an office worker with one of the government offices in Kawempe and was going to spend the weekend with her boyfriend or family elsewhere. There was no wedding band on her ring finger, so I imagined a boyfriend would be in the picture. That was how wild my childish imagination was.

"Sorry, I was …" I trailed off. I had no reason to give my sister.

"You're always staring at people every time you are sent on errands. I'm going to report you to Mama. She has been waiting for you, and she sent me to look for you. She is worried, and you're here…"

"Nooo!" I cut in. "Please don't tell Mama…" I pleaded as I ran to catch up with her. I didn't know I had taken too long, and I didn't want my mom to stop sending me on errands. Those were the times I got to explore my neighborhood and expand my world view by watching how people spoke and behaved. The things I learned from my observation of them groomed me for when I became an adult. Who would have known that the feisty and inquisitive girl who skipped more than she walked as a pre-teen girl, and who always had a big smile for everyone would someday become the beauty queen of her country and the influencer she is today. I will share how that happened in subsequent chapters, and it's a story of first having a vision of what you want in your heart and then working to see it come into your hand. If you want it badly enough and you work it at intentionally, you will get it.

While the experiences I garnered from helping my mom sell and earn a living taught me to be independent at an early age, it caused a strain between my dad and I for a long time. I realized that he was supposed to have provided many of the things my mom went out of her way to get for us. All the businesses she did and stress that she went through as a single mother could have been avoidable, if he was there to support us. Even as I write this book, my relationship with him is still evolving, but I have outgrown a lot of things.

As a young child, I blamed him for everything that happened in his marriage to my mom and for all the hardship we went through. But as an adult, I see things differently now. I understand that certain things happen that a person might not be in control of and that some circumstances are just meant to be the way they are. Once I understood that, I forgave him. I also acknowledge the fact that since I didn't have a strong relationship with him from my childhood, it affects the way I relate with him today. We talk just once or twice in a month, but I do love him. He's the only parent I have, and I look so much like him. He's quite tall, and I believe I got my tallness from him. He's also a handsome man, and it's not surprising that women swooned over him all those years ago. But, I can see that he's sorry for the choices he made and subsequent mistakes as a young man and wishes he could turn back the hands of time.

One thing I'm always grateful for though is that what I lacked in relating with him, was made up for in greater measures in my relationship with my mom. My mom and I were very close while she was alive. I literally went everywhere with her. We slept on the same bed, ate our meals together, and she took me to school until I could go by myself. She was always ready to listen to anything I had to say, and she taught me about life as we lived it together. We had a very strong connection, so it was a big blow to me when she passed away suddenly. She died at a time when I was just coming into my own and becoming the woman I wanted to be.

Whenever my imaginations went wild, I would paint pictures of the type of future I wanted to have. Even though she knew those things were farfetched because of our condition and standard of living at the time, she didn't discourage me from thinking my thoughts. She didn't discourage me from dreaming. Somehow, even with the minimal exposure and education she had, she understood the power of dreams in seeing the things a person desires come to fulfilment. She knew that you had to first see it in your mind's eye, before it could grow in your heart and finally be in your hands.

As for my siblings, I separated from the older ones when I was about 9 years except my immediate elder sister. So, I didn't have a strong connection with them. We just came together during family events and holidays and greeted one another. There was no hugging, laughing or mushiness that accompanies relating with a sibling. This was partly due to the fact that we lived apart for most of the year and didn't keep in touch in any way.

Going away

After the celebrations and holidays, everyone went back to living with the parent they've always lived with. Even though my dad asked me to live with him a few times, I refused. My mom was my most favorite person in the whole world, so I preferred to live with her over living with anyone else. But, all of that changed one December when my extended family came together for the holidays. My dad's elder sister also came for the celebrations with her family and while she was there, the adults had a family meeting. It was common practice for the parents to do a review of the past year and take stock of how everyone is doing. This practice was started generations before them and followed by generations after them. It ensured that no family member was left behind without proper care and guidance in life. It is a good practice to adopt in families, if you ask me; especially in families where there are marital separations and stepfather, stepmother and children situations.

So it was, that at the family meeting held in December of the year I turned 16, it was decided that I would no longer live with my mom. I was to move away to go and live with my aunt. I remember how stunned I was when my mom broke the news to me and how she quietly sat with me as I processed the news. I saw the pain and helplessness in her eyes and knew that it was something she could do nothing about.

"I don't want to leave you, Mama" I whimpered, as I lay my head on her laps.

"I know, my Olive…" she whispered in reply, caressing my hair and looking into the distance.

It was dusk that day and while my cousins ran around in the courtyard of my granduncle's house where we held the celebrations that year, I sat with my mom in despair, unsure of what the new year and future held for me. My aunt was well to do, was more enlightened and lived in a big city, and as a teenager, I should have been attracted to the prospects of a better life than I had living with my mom, but I didn't want it. I had anticipated that the change would be an unwelcome one for me, and I was right.

At the end of the holidays, I packed my bag and went with my aunt. Saying our goodbyes was even worse than I thought it would be. I was 16 years old and had never been separated from my mom since I was born. It felt like I was being torn away from the familiar to the unfamiliar. I clung to my mom, and shed tears as she spoke to me.

"Make sure you behave well, Olive (that was the nickname she called me). Do your chores and always be a good girl. Study hard too; your aunt is taking you away to give you a good education, so make the most of it, you hear? Remember all your dreams and all the things you want to become. Hmmm? When you are educated, you will become all of them, do you understand?" She said, her eyes shining with tears. She had always been a strong woman and I knew she would not cry openly, but I was already a mess.

"That's enough now, let's go. I don't want to travel late in the day" my aunt cut in impatiently.

Her family were already seated in the car, and her husband was at the wheel ready to drive off. I glanced at my dad who stood a few feet from us, arms crossed over his chest. He didn't say a word.

I hugged my mom one last time and got into the back seat with my aunt's two young children; clutching my travel bag to my chest. I was miserable, but there was nothing I could do about it. There was nothing my mom could do about it either. In the part of Africa where I come from, a child belongs to his father; therefore, decisions concerning his life, education and future can only be made by the father or members of the father's family. The mother has no say in it. Even though my parents were separated and there was no plan for reconciliation, every time the family gathered for events or festivities, my mom was expected to be there to play her part as a mother to children in that family.

We soon got to my aunt's home, and I quickly adjusted to living there. It was a large compound with a four-bedroom house in the center. The following week after I arrived there, my aunt enrolled me in a high school. Being in that school was one of the highlights of my stay in that city. My happiest moments were when I was in school, with my classmates and favorite teachers. I was brilliant and intelligent at answering questions in class, and my teachers soon took notice of me. My first few weeks at school were interesting, but as my chores and duties in the house increased, I began to concentrate less on school work. After about four weeks of living there, I no longer felt like a member of the family; I felt more like a maid. Even though there was a maid in the house, I felt like I was being used to do the extra house work. I cleaned the house every day and did the family's laundry on weekends.

Many times I'd feel so exhausted that I sometimes dozed off during lessons in class. Going through those experience made me long for my mom and my sister. My mom didn't have a large house, and we did all the chores together. Plus, there was warmth and laughter in our home; that was something that was lacking in my aunt's home. She was a strict person who expected everything she dictated to be done the way she dictated them. She always wanted her home to be spic and span; no dirt or litter even with her little children around. She expected members of her household to behave in certain ways, to dress in certain ways and to eat breakfast and dinner together as a family. She had zero tolerance for any behavior that was different from what she dictated or expected, and her word was final on every issue. After living with her for three months, I understood why even my dad could not stand up to her on many occasions and especially concerning me going to live with her; which I clearly didn't want. I remember when she found out that I had a boyfriend. It was about 6 months after I started to live with her. It was not a serious relationship; the boy was just someone I liked and had grown quite close to, but my aunt would not hear it. She ranted and stormed the boy's house warning him to leave me alone, or else she would deal with him. Then, she restricted me from going out with my friends. Immediately I closed from school, I was to go home directly.

It was an embarrassing time for me, and I felt bad that the poor boy was also being embarrassed on my account. But, I reasoned that she wanted me to focus on my studies and not get distracted. So, I accepted all her restrictions, but was surprised to later find that all she was protecting from in the outside world, would later come to me inside her home. What happened and how did it happen? Come with me as I reveal it all.

CHAPTER 3
THE LOVE LETTERS

In all I was going through at home when I began to live with my aunt, the only place I found solace was at school. My school life was quiet interesting, and I loved going to school. I don't know if it was intentional but more often than not, my mom had enrolled my sister and I in mission schools. These mission schools were run by different denominations of the Christian religion. There was a time I attended a Catholic school. At another time, I attended an Anglican school and an Adventist school as well. It was as if I was exploring the different denominations as a student. Now, I understand that my mom put us in those schools because the church bodies are thought to run a comprehensive and holistic educational system.

Apart from having seasoned teachers in employment who teach students well, they also see to the spiritual development of students by teaching them salient truths from the Bible. These were my experiences as I attended these schools. Apart from learning, I made friends from different walks of life, and my relationships with them prepared me for the life I embarked upon as an adult. After my high school education, I did an Advanced Certificate course for two years at a Muslim school, and it was a different experience altogether.

In Uganda at that time, we had O levels from Senior 1 to Senior 4. I did Senior 4 at my aunt's place and then graduated to A levels. At the Muslim school, I offered Arts subjects: Language, History, Visual Art, Christianity and other subjects and being a different religion, I came in contact with people who had different belief systems about God and who did things slightly differently from how I did them. I made a lot of friends there too, in fact my two best friends are from there. However as much as I loved school, I had a tough time with certain subjects. My two favorite subjects were Literature in English and English language, and my love for languages inspired me to study my mother tongue, which is called Luganda. We also took Entrepreneurial courses, which were designed to teach students different skillsets and equip them with the basics of starting businesses, along with the career path they would choose. But, as good as the idea seemed, I chose not to take the Entrepreneurial course because of the teachers. Those teachers were the meanest teachers I have ever come across. I don't know if it was an unspoken agreement among them, but all of them were mean to us students. They would give us assignments and project works, and if we so much as approached them to ask questions so as to get a clearer understanding of what we needed to do, they would send us away like pests. It was truly disheartening for us teenagers at that time, but we knew that if we reported them to the school authorities, it would cause more problems for us. I knew it wasn't the proper way to treat students, because we had other teachers who were approachable and ready to help us whenever we went to them; so I did what was within my control. I made a choice and dropped the course. It was quite a bold thing to do because other students were afraid to incur the wrath of the Entrepreneurial teachers, but I was tired of going through hell at their hands.

I wasn't going to study what I was paying for, under duress. It didn't seem fair to me. It was also from that point that I began to learn and practice what it meant to stand up for what I believe in, no matter whose ox is gored.

Although the Entrepreneurial course experience happened many years ago, now I'm in the midst of finalizing my degree and ironically it's a business course. I'm doing really well in it, and I can't think of a better course that I would have studied except business. Shortly before I started the business course, I studied journalism in 2014, but I can't say that I was really vested in it and I didn't see as much opportunities in it as I see in business. With all I'm learning in my business course, I daresay that everyone needs to study a business course. Having said that, away from the teachers who made learning tough for me, I had many favorite teachers, and they were mostly teachers of religion. Those teachers were good listeners and patient people; they had good understanding of the way the mind of a young person works and the many questions that run around in it. Many times, I would sit with them and ask questions about God and the truthfulness of His existence. They didn't see me as one who was asking questions just to poke holes in their beliefs. Rather, they saw me as a young person who has a deep mind and fertile imagination and who did more critical thinking about issues than her mates did. I know this because they said it to me many times. On the flip side, things have changed a lot in the educational space because while I had physical access to all my teachers as a feisty high school girl, now that I'm in university, I study online most of the time. I have never met most of my teachers, yet I have a long list of amazing people who teach me and model what it means to be a person of value to me.

Going through school

It is important to mention that my high school experience wasn't all book work, I had memorable experiences in sports. Being taller than my age gave me more advantage than my peers because I got to engage in sporting activities in each class I got to. First, it was in netball. I was so good at it that there was a day I scored over 22 goals in just one play. It was fun to dribble and dunk players who were shorter than I and watch the dismay on their faces as I shot the ball into the basket. I was almost signed up for the National Netball Team of Uganda, but something came up and it didn't sail through. Perhaps if it had, I wouldn't have become a beauty queen and I wouldn't be inspired to write my life's story. But, this is my life now and this is who I am, and there are no regrets whatsoever. In university, I also did sports. I played basketball and was on the Queens team, and I loved every minute of it. I also did a lot of volunteering activities in university. Apart from getting to meet teams from other universities and interacting with them, playing basketball is one of the ways I keep fit. Running around the pitch, jumping, stretching and dunking keeps my heart healthy and my arm and thigh muscles toned.

Some of the worst days I had as a student was when I was in junior high school. I was still living with my mom and because she was solely responsible for my sister and I, sometimes she could not afford to pay my school fees on time. And, the rule at the school then was that after a few weeks of defaulting in paying school fees, the student would be sent back home from school. Sometimes on the afternoon assembly, the Principal would announce that students who still owe the school should not bother to come to school the following day. But, I didn't listen. I just couldn't imagine staying away from school. For me, it felt like an abomination. I thought of all the school work I would miss out on; my friends that I would miss playing with, and the overall camaraderie of going to school. So on a particular day, even though I had told my mom what the Principal instructed, I woke early and got ready for school.

"Olive, didn't you tell me the Principal told you not to come to school if you're owing school fees?" She asked.

"Yes" I answered.

"So, what are you doing?"

"I'm going to school, Mom. I can't just stay here and wait. I want to learn. I will plead with him when I get to school. I know you will get the money, but I will be missing a lot if I just stay at home," I said as I lifted my rucksack onto my shoulders. My mom knew how determined I could be when it came to matters concerning school, so she didn't stand in my way.

That day, I went to school and as if fate smiled on me, the Principal didn't go round the classes to send any student out. Many parents had showed up that day to pay their children's school fees, so it made him relax a little. And like I predicted, my mom got the money to pay my schools fees the following week and I stayed on that school. That incident taught me something about taking chances and being decisive. Even though I had been sent home for non-payment of school fees, I knew how important education was and how much I would miss if I stayed home for even one day. So, I decided that I was going to appeal to the Principal. Was I scared to face him? No! I only knew that it could play out in one of two ways. He could look at me and tell me to go home and wait till my mom could afford to pay my fees, or he could look beyond the teenage girl standing in his office and see a child who didn't want to miss out on having an education. I hoped the second option was what would happen. Thankfully, I didn't have to use any option.

That doggedness and resilience followed me through junior school, high school and critical points in my life such as when I decided to apply for the Miss Uganda Beauty Pageant. I will share more of what made me decide to participate in a pageant of that magnitude and how I emerged the winner, in subsequent chapters, but one of my most memorable days in life was when I was given a warm welcome as Miss Uganda, at my university in Dubai. It was so heartwarming to see men and women, young and old give me a standing ovation as I walked to the podium. It was more spectacular to me because they were people from different, races, cultures and religions and there they were clapping for me, Oliver Nakakande—Miss Uganda 2019—who had come to study at their university. That day, I had a whole session to myself as I gave speeches and spoke about my organization, as well as the projects I was working on. I told them how I was slated to attend the Miss World pageant and represent my country, Uganda. It was refreshing to tell them about the advocacy and causes that I had started to work on. I spoke about the Stop Teenage Pregnancy project and what I was doing with the Miss Uganda team to stop the menace and ensure that young girls stay in school and get an education. I spoke about the clean water projects and our drive to provide clean water and sanitation to impoverished families in Uganda. After my speech that day, I got some support and created more awareness about my dreams and plans for girls and women back home in Uganda. That day, a good friend of mine, Naicy gave me a book as gift. The book is titled Becoming and was written by Michelle Obama, the one-time First Lady of the United States of America. She gave me a journal as well, and a note wishing me all the best and hoping that one day I'll get to share my story with the world. Naicy is one of the people who inspired me to start reading and enlarge my knowledge frontiers through books. That was a huge highlight of my university education life, and I'm grateful that the crown of Miss Uganda 2019 provided that platform for me.

My uncle's letters

Yet, with all these wonderful memories, there was an unpleasant side to my teenhood. It was something that threatened to destroy all the dreams and plans I had for my future. That experience reminds me of a story I once read about. It's the story of a broken vessel. The servants of a certain king used vessels to fetch water from the stream for the king's table. Among the vessels the servants used, one was broken. Each time the servants brought the vessels back from the stream, the broken vessels got to the king's table empty. All the water had leaked out of it through the cracks in it, during the journey back from the stream. This vessel began to feel unworthy. It wanted to be like the other vessels that were perfect, fetched water from the stream to the king's table and served him. It wanted an opportunity to serve the king. "If only I can be perfect like the other vessels," it thought, "then my life will be useful and the king will find me worthy as well."

What this vessel didn't realize is that along the path from the stream to the palace, beautiful flowers had begun to grow. It was such a beautiful sight to behold that everyone wondered how it had happened. It was soon discovered that the water that leaked from the broken vessel had watered the earth and caused the beautiful flowers to grow, thereby beautifying the pathway to the king's palace.

This story moved me to tears because at the time I was going through unpleasant experiences in my teenhood, I felt like that broken vessel. I felt unworthy because I thought the only thing I could be useful for was to be a toy in the hands of a man. I didn't see a way of escape, and that thought alone demoralized me. It adversely affected my mental health, and my school grades suffered. I had no one to confide in and even if I did, who would believe the words of a 16-year-old girl over that of a 40something-year-old man. Who would believe that the person I called 'uncle' would think of having an affair with me; his niece.

It all started when I was preparing for my final examinations out of high school. In Uganda, it is common culture that when a student is preparing for such an examination, friends and family members can send a success card to wish him or her success in the examination and promotion to the next phase of their lives. My friends were excited to receive success cards from their family members and they often showed me their cards. It made me envious of them because no one had sent me a success card. My mom and sister were far away, and they didn't even know I was to write an examination.

Then, my own success letter came. It was a beautiful card with beautiful colors and flowers printed all over it. I was so happy because it was the first card I would receive that academic year. I wasn't expecting any one from home, so it was nice to see that someone else apart from my mom and sister cared about me and wished me well. The sender definitely wished me all the best in my examination, but inside it was also a love letter that told me how much he loved me and how he felt for me and how I shouldn't tell anyone about it. What? I was confused. The sender was my uncle. What did he mean? He is my dad's cousin, so I referred to him as 'uncle'. He was also by extension my aunt's cousin and lived about three cities away from where I lived with her family. Whenever he had to work at the branch of his office that was in the city where we lived, he stayed at my aunt's house. So, even though I was happy in his presence and thanked him when he gave the success letter to me, by the time I had sat on my bed and read the love letter, I was dumfounded. I immediately lost the trust I had in him and in its place, I felt disgust. How could he do this? Didn't he know who I was? Didn't he know my relationship to him? Even if I wasn't related to him, was it right for him a 40-something-year-old man to prey on a 16-year-old girl that way? I might not have known many things about life at that time, but I knew that what he had done was not proper. I started to see him in a totally different light and feared being alone with him. He was already married at the time and had three children? That made it even worse for me because I thought, "If he could think of doing this with me, it meant he had probably cheated on his wife with other women." And, my regard for him just dwindled more.

So, I acted as if what he had done wasn't a big deal but deep down in my heart, I was struggling with the fact that it was actually happening. I also didn't want my aunt to find out anything, and I didn't plan to send him a reply even though in his letter, he had asked me to tell him how I feel about him. When I didn't send him a reply, he wrote another letter. He wrote three letters in total, and I kept all of them just for reference purposes in case I would need to show them to someone one day. The second one was a followup on the first letter he had written in the success card, because I had begun to avoid him. I didn't want to talk to him, and I didn't want to even cross his path. He used to visit my aunt's home and spend two days in a month whenever he needed to work in the city, so I was careful to avoid him during those two days. But on the day he gave me the second love letter, he wasn't expected in the house. He lied to my aunt that he had come on an impromptu visit with one of his bosses and just stopped to say hi to us. I knew he was lying because he left my aunt outside where they had sat talking for a while and came into my bedroom to give me the letter.

My cousins and I shared an open bedroom that had no door, so anyone could walk in. I was lying on the bed alone and reading a novel when he snuck up on me. I was surprised that he was suddenly in the room with me, and I showed it in the way I recoiled and shifted away from him towards the headboard. "How're you, Olly?" He asked, with a smile on his face.

I didn't smile back because I felt so much disdain for him.

Taking things further

I don't know if he got my unspoken message, because he hurriedly dropped the letter beside the novel that had fallen off my hands onto the bed and went out of the room. My heart was beating fast and for many minutes, I felt like crying. I missed my mom so much during that period, because she is the only person I could have told and who could have told me what to do or handled the situation well. She was a calm and sensible woman, who taught me how to wise and tactful in dealing with others. I know she wouldn't have made a huge scene of the matter because it involved a family member, but I was certain she would have warned my uncle to stay away from me or else she would tell his wife and show her all his love letters. For a long time, the thought of doing that crossed my mind but I was afraid of executing the plan. I wasn't sure how he would react and I didn't want any problem or quarrel to start in the family on my account; it was bad enough that I was living in a place I didn't want to live. My hands were tied, or so I thought. After he left the room, I picked up the envelope. It wasn't flat like an ordinary letter envelope; there was something in it. When I opened it, it contained a phone, a sim card, money, and a letter. In the letter, he professed his undying love to me and instructed that I should activate the phone and call him, so that he could talk with me and explain his plans for us.

I was so angry at him for taking things further, but after some thought, I realized that it was a blessing in disguise. So, rather than call him, I called my mom and my sister. I was so happy to hear from them, that we swapped stories of what had been happening in our lives all year long. I didn't tell my mom how I gad gotten a phone to call her, because I didn't want her to panic. I knew that in the next couple of months I would be done with my examinations, and I could go back to her. So, I planned to play cool until then. Then, something changed. He was transferred to our city to handle a project for his company for three months, and that meant that he would stay in my aunt's house for that period of time. It was a turbulent period for me because it meant that I would see him almost every day.

To make matters worse, there were days he didn't go to work at all and whenever I got back home from school, there he was smiling at me from the garden table where he usually sat outside. Whenever he knew that we would be alone, he would sneak behind me, caress my body and tell me how much he loved me. I usually shunned him and moved to another part of the house. After about two weeks of him doing it, it began to affect my psyche. I began to feel worthless and taken advantage of. I knew he didn't love me. I was smart enough to understand that he just wanted to have sex with me. I also knew that the only way he could do that was if he raped me; there was no way I would willingly give in to his sweet words.

He was also a smart man. He treated my cousins and I the same way, so no one suspected anything. He wasn't as strict as my aunt, so naturally, the children loved to have him around. He would buy sweets, chocolates and biscuits on his way home every day, so the children looked forward to seeing him. Even the maid was not left out of his generosity. He usually bought bananas and groundnuts for her. So, it was hard to know if he was giving me any preference; you couldn't tell from his actions.

When I saw how increasingly difficult it was becoming to stay away from him, I knew it was time to activate an escape plan. If I didn't, he would rape me and probably lie that I seduced him, and I wouldn't be able to do anything about it. I had read too many novels to learn how situations like that played out. I was determined not to be a victim. So, what did I do?

CHAPTER 4
THE ESCAPE PLAN

I began to put plans in place to run away. If I couldn't stop what my uncle was doing to me, at least I could get away from him.

My final examination was fast approaching, and it was the perfect chance for me to run away. I had been brought to live with my aunt, because my parents thought that she could afford to give me a good education. I did get a good education from living at her house, so I wasn't going to let a man who didn't know his right from his left corrupt me and destroy my life. Initially, his attitude towards me (especially whenever I was alone with him) depressed me a lot. I struggled to understand how easy it was for him to tap my buttocks and make lewd comments to me even when he knew we are relations. I figured that things like that were usually acceptable between people who weren't related and who could get married, but I was wrong. As young as I was, I began to learn that people didn't only do what was right; they could do what they knew was wrong too, as long as it caught their fancy.

As time went on, I noticed something strange about my uncle. Whenever he visited and related with me where other members of the family were, he related to me as a father would to his daughter. But in reality, he was a monster. A monster who didn't think twice before taking advantage of his own niece. Of all the women he could have, why did he choose me? If he wanted to have a mistress, he could look for an adult woman to love and have sex with; not a naive 16-year-old. These questions milled around in my head and fought hard to find expression. In my bid to find answers to them, I did research about his behavior and found many stories related to abuse of teenage girls. I found that apart from the ideology that young girls are safer to have unprotected sex with, men who abuse them do so because they are able to control the girls and feel powerful. They also sometimes abuse girls in order to manage or act out difficult emotions that they may be going through. Where the abuse goes on among a group, a man may do it to gain status in the eyes of other men.

On the whole, I found that children are usually targeted for sexual abuse simply because they're more vulnerable than adults. And, that was the case with me. He knew the situation of my parent's marriage and knew that I was living in a place I didn't want to be. He also knew that my aunt was strict and perhaps thought that I would jump into his arms when he played on my emotions and told me he loved me. But, he was wrong. I might have been living with a strict aunt and lacking the comfort and freedom that I would have had if I were living with my parents, but I wasn't love-starved. I knew that my mom and my sister loved me and wanted the best for me. They told me every time I had the opportunity to speak with them on phone. During those times, I told them how I was coping and they filled me in with what was happening back home. So, even though we were miles apart, my love tank was full to overflowing. I didn't need a man to tell me he loved me for me to believe that I was lovable. My family's love was enough and for that I'll remain ever grateful. That experience taught me how important it is for parents to love their children and constantly express it to them in words and actions. That was one of the things that kept me from falling into my uncle's trap.

Having understood that fact, I resolved to stay away from him as much as possible. Whenever he was in town, I made up excuses to be out of the house as much as I could. I told my aunt that as final year students, we were required to be at school for extra tutorials in the evenings and on Saturdays. Even on Sundays, I put up excuses that we were told to come to school to observe study periods so that there would be no distractions from family members or television. I told all these lies just so I could stay out of the house and away from him. But, there were times I couldn't be away from the house, and he took advantage of those times.

One day, he told me to make tea for him. I made it, put it on the dining table and called out to him that it was ready. He responded by saying I should bring it to him in the bedroom. I thought it was weird, because I had never taken tea to him in the bedroom. Besides, my aunt was a stickler for proper behavior. No one ate anything in the bedrooms; all foods were eaten on the dining table. I knew these things but I couldn't object to his order and my aunt who could (if she saw me do it) wasn't at home. So, I got to the bedroom and put the tea cup on a small table next to the bed he was sitting on.

As I turned to leave, he forcefully grabbed my hand and pulled me to his body. I was so scared that I didn't know what to do momentarily. When I recovered enough to realize that I was in danger, I began to struggle with him. His grip was firm and hard on me being a heavily built man himself, so my efforts were feeble; but I didn't stop. Then, when I saw that he didn't loosen his hold, I began to cry and beg him to let me go. That was when he turned me to face him, looked me in the eyes and started to say, "Look, it's going to be fine. You're going to be fine, you'll enjoy it. I promise you…" I couldn't believe he was looking at me, his niece and saying those things to me. I couldn't imagine how he could do it. By that time, I had started to wail, but no one was coming to save me. I had left my cousins playing in the garden, but they could have gone next door to play with our neighbors. The maid was also out running errands, so I was at his mercy.

As these thoughts ran through my mind, as I heard him say again, "I know you're not a virgin, you've done this before, haven't you. Come on, it's not going to be painful, you'll like it. I promise to be gentle…"

Suddenly, it felt like I was hearing all he was saying from someplace very far away. I heard myself resisting him and telling him I was 16 years old and still a virgin, but he didn't seem to hear me. At that moment, my whole life flashed before my eyes. It was as if someone switched on a screen and showed me a glimpse of what my life would look like if I let him have his way. I knew I was getting too weak to fight him, and my arms had begun to ache from him pinning me to his body for several minutes. I had cried so much, but my tears didn't move him. I knew that if he raped me, it would never stop. I also knew that if I became pregnant, my family would never consent to me having an abortion and my life would change forever. I saw my dreams of becoming a successful woman crushed. I saw my life as an inspiration to girls and women fly out of the window. I saw my hopes of giving my mom the life she deserves, dash into pieces and at the point I lost it. With my last ounce of strength, I threw my head back and screamed "NOOOOOOO!" at the top of my voice. As I screamed, I shook my head and my body and vibrated with intense fury. Till today, I don't know what came over me, but whatever it was, I'm grateful to it because he pushed me away. The push was so sudden that I felt on the floor. But even in that fall, I had presence of mind to scramble to my feet and run to safety. I was blind with tears and just ran out of the house. I wanted to be as far away from him as possible. I remember running to a spot not far from my school. It was a shade created by three orange trees, and my friends and I sometimes sat under it to rest and talk on our way from school. We also plucked oranges whenever we saw ripe ones and ate them as we talked. I don't know why I chose that spot, but I sat on one part of the buttress roots rising out of the ground, put my face on my palms and cried out my frustrations. I felt a little bit safe under that shade, because my friends and I had created good memories there. Sadly, I couldn't say the same about my aunt's house.

As the gentle breeze from the trees wafted around me, I felt a strange sense of victory. It was as if that was the worst my uncle could do to me and from that day, my escape plan began to form in my head.

Staying away

After that encounter, I was always on my guard around him. If before that day, I tried to be polite and respectful to him, in spite of him constantly tapping my buttocks, after that incident, there was always a scowl on my face for him. He noticed the change in my behavior towards him, and tried to make things better by buying gifts for me, but I didn't accept them. Whenever he bought snacks and shared to all the children in the presence of my aunt, I collected them but threw them away later. I swore never to have anything to do with again in my life, and I couldn't wait to run away from there. Once, when he brought some boxes home, he told me to carry them to his bedroom. When it remained one box in the living room, he stayed back in the bedroom and told me to go and bring the box to him. I had an inkling of what his intentions were, so I was ready to protect myself. I had promised myself that I would no longer be caught in such a vulnerable situation as I had been with him before. So when I entered the bedroom, I made sure to leave the door ajar, quickly set the box down on the bedside stool and backed away from him. I did that because I didn't want to turn my back to him at any point in time. If I did, he could grab me from behind and overpower me again. After all, once beaten twice shy.

"Olly, come and …" he started to say but I had already fled from the bedroom.

My aunt and the maid had gone grocery shopping that day, leaving me to look after my cousins. So, I knew it would be an opportunity for him to try to lure me into his bedroom again. I had anticipated his actions and already planned how I would stall them. After I fled from his bedroom, I made sure I stayed in the garden watching my cousins play on the grass. I reasoned that if I were in the open and with my cousins, he would not try to touch me. I also made sure that I sat facing the entrances and exits of the house, so that he wouldn't be able to sneak up on me.

Doing all of these planning and safeguarding regularly eventually began to take a toll on my academics. I became a shadow of myself. Gone was the feisty and ever-smiling tall, slim Oliver. In her place was this fidgety, moody and easily irritable girl, who snapped at anyone who tried to play with her. My smile disappeared and in its place, I wore a permanent frown. I became angry with everyone. Why was I going through this? Why did my life have to be this difficult? Wasn't it enough that my parent's marriage had broken down, and our family had split up? Wasn't that enough punishment? Why did I have to go through this sexual harassment as well?

I had no one to ask these questions, so I became bitter. I lost concentration in school, and my grades dropped terribly. Initially, I was doing well when I first arrived at the school, even though I had transferred from a school in another district. It was a different school system from what I was used to, but because I was determined to succeed and make my mom proud, I put in my best and did the work required. I had made friends, gotten used to the system and was doing well academically, until the sexual harrassment began to happen. I was constantly exhausted from the fact that I wasn't getting enough sleep, because I was watching my back all night. At that time, the work project that he came to do in town had been extended, so he was staying at my aunt's house all weeklong. Sometimes, he travelled to visit his family over the weekends and sometimes he didn't. I was also afraid that someone might find the love letters that I hidden away. Like I mentioned before, the bedroom I shared with one of my cousins had no door, and there were no lockers or drawers to put anything for safekeeping. I was just living in a nightmare. I also became an emotional wreck, because I didn't want to tell anyone what was happening; even though I had a good friend living next door. I knew that if I did, it would only be a matter of time before other people knew about it. I didn't want to be the cause of any problem in the family. I just told myself that I had a little more time to endure the unpleasant situation before I would be safe with my mom and sister again. As a teenager, it was hard for me to even think that by telling anyone other than my mom what was happening, I could be saved. So, I thought that if I kept it to myself and got out of the situation unscathed, the matter would stay with me forever. And, maybe it would be revealed when I'm ready.

Whenever I lied to my aunt that we had classes over the weekend, just so I could be out of the house and away from my uncle, I sometimes went to see my boyfriend. We would sit under the shade of the orange tree and just talk and laugh and eat candy. He knew that I liked candy, so he always bought some for me whenever we planned to see one another. We were young and just loved talking to each other and laughing. I didn't even know what a boyfriend was for, but I know I loved spending time with him. Apart from my female friend who lived next door, my boyfriend was the only other bright spot in my otherwise sad life. He didn't know it at the time (because I didn't tell him what was happening), but he helped me to forget that I was living with a monster. For a long time, my aunt didn't suspect that I had been lying to her. She knew that the class I was in required us to do extra revisions for our examination, so she didn't really bother much about my constant absence from the house. But, she eventually found out. That day, I lost track of time and set out for home later than I should have. Unknown to me, she had waited for me around the corner that led to our house and saw me walking home with my friends.

I remember that night as clearly as if it happened last night. My boyfriend and I had been talking and enjoying each other's company at our usual spot and before we knew it, it had gotten really late. We were with two other male friends, and our conversation was so interesting that we all lost track of time. When I looked at the time and jumped up to go home, they all escorted me. We had just rounded the corner to my aunt's house, when her voice boomed at us. She was so mad!

"Where are you coming from, Oliver?"

I stopped immediately, and my boyfriend ran into me from behind. We almost fell to the ground, but managed to steady ourselves to see my aunt standing arms akimbo in front of us.

"Err… I err… I was…" I stammered.

"You were what!" She roared at me.

"So, this is what you've been doing now eh? Dating boys now? "Staying out this late?" She asked, barely allowing me to answer one question before asking another.

"No Aunty, I was …"

"You were what? By the time I'm done with you, you'll be sorry." She raged.

And with that, she ordered me to put my bag in the house and follow her to my boyfriend's house. She knew where he lived, so she marched there that night. When she got there, she complained to his mom that her son was spoiling me and that she didn't want me to see him again. She also called the parents of the two other boys and said the same thing. Then, she warned me never to associate with them again. That put me in a difficult situation because they were not just my friends; we were classmates and would definitely see one another in school everyday. Although, I didn't have to bear the awkward situation for long, because my moment of escape was very close.

Running away

I remember the day I ran away; it was one that I had carefully planned for, for a very long time. The moment I got my examination timetable, I began to mark dates and knew that I would finish my examination around midday on a certain day. That would give me enough time to come back home, pick my bag and travel to my maternal uncle's house before anyone realized it. I had packed my bags in such a way that no one would sense that I planned on leaving the house. I had some beautiful items that were important to me but which were too large for me to carry. So, I packed them neatly and gave them to my friend next door. I told her I'd be back to collect them, but I had to take some other items home first. I didn't tell her I was running away or anything, I just played it cool. With that, I had just one small bag to travel with.

When I got back from school, the maid served lunch. I remember very well that the meal that was served that day was Matoke. It is a local meal in Uganda made with green bananas that are boiled and mashed. That day, it was served with groundnuts and dry fish stew. It is a delicious meal that I loved to eat any day, but that day I didn't have the appetite to eat anything. I just wanted to get away from there. I couldn't afford to let my guards down or let anyone notice that I had planned to run away. Ironically, the whole family was at home on that day except my aunt. My uncle was somewhere in the house; he didn't go to work that day.

Usually, when a person plans to run away from danger to safety, he does it when no one would be around to stop him. But, not me. I couldn't afford to wait till the following week when all the adults would go to work, the children would go to school, and I didn't have to go to school anymore. I had planned to move that day and nothing was going to stop me; not even my favorite Matoke. When I was ready to leave, I opened the back door and put my bag outside by the hedge of flowers. I had planned to wait until they were seated to eat lunch. That way, I would have gone far before they noticed my absence.

As I picked my bag and started to walk towards the gate, the maid came out to put something in the waste bin and saw me.

"Where are you going?" She called out to me. I stopped and turned to look at her, but didn't walk back to meet her. I didn't want to lie, so I said to her:

"When aunty comes back, tell her not to look for me; I'm safe."

I told her the truth indirectly, because that statement meant,

"I'm going away from here, and I'm not coming back."

I really didn't care at that point if she was going to go into the house and report to my uncle. I was done with my examination and running away from all the mess and heartache I had endured for almost one year. Nothing was going to hold me back there anymore. I had put my plans in place and was already executing them. In fact, I knew my plans would work, because I was already at the final stage.

So, I told the maid the truth indirectly and walked away quickly before she could ask me more questions.

Luckily for me, I found a taxi almost immediately and that was how I ran away. My escape plan was successful. When I got to my maternal uncle's house, his family welcomed me and I was happy. I hadn't seen them in a long time, and it felt good to be hugged and touched and smiled at. I told them that I just finished my examination and wanted to spend some time with them before I travelled home to my mom and sister. My story held until later at night when my uncle began to receive frantic phone calls. My aunt was looking for me, and she had called my mom to ask if I was with her. My mom guessed what I had done and called her brother immediately. She knew that his house was not far from the town my aunt lived and if there was any place I would go to first if I had the chance, it would be his house.

The news had spread among my family members that I had run away from my aunt's house without saying goodbye.

Then, my uncle woke me up from sleep and asked what happened. I started to cry as I explained everything and showed him proof of all the letters that my uncle had written to me. I could see the anger rise in my uncle's eyes, but I begged him not to tell my mom. I wanted to tell myself when I reached home. After spending two days of carefree laughter and happiness with my uncle's family, I finally travelled home.

When I got home, I told my mom all that I went through, and both of us cried. From that day, she swore never to give us away to any relative, come rain or sunshine. As for my aunt, she was mad at me for a long time because I didn't tell her the reason I ran away. I didn't trust her to believe me because my uncle is her favorite cousin, and it would be my word against his.

CHAPTER 5
STARTING OVER

The truth is, I didn't intend to cause any trouble in the family in spite of what my uncle did to me. In fact, that was the reason I planned my escape before he would get the opportunity to rape me and cause irreparable damage. It was also why I begged my maternal uncle not to tell my mom what had happened. I wanted to tell her face to face by myself. When I got home, I almost chickened out of telling her the whole story because it was quite unbelievable. Every single person that I told what happened to me found it hard to believe that my uncle didn't rape me. It was a situation that everybody believed that I had been endangered and probably raped but wasn't telling the truth, so I had to convince them that nothing happened. I explained all the things I had done to avoid being alone with him in the house and how I had planned my escape for the last day of my examination. If I hadn't taken time to explain these things, I'm certain my uncle would have reported him to the Police. But, I'm glad he believed me because it would have caused a serious problem in the family.

When I told my mom what had happened and showed her all the letters my uncle had written to me, she reacted exactly how I thought she would react. She was so angry and asked if he had raped me. I told her that he hadn't and had a hard time convincing her that I was okay. I shudder to think of what she would have done if he had succeeded in raping me.

My dad, on the other hand didn't react in any spectacular way when he heard what happened to me, and I don't blame him for it. He was not really present in my life, so me going away to live with my aunt or coming back home in the circumstances I did, was none of his business. He didn't care that much about where I was or what was happening in my life, because I was raised largely by my mom and other people around us. My dad was just somebody I knew was my dad. He was not concerned about the important issues of my life: my education, my welfare etc.; we just had a weird relationship between us. Apart from him, no other person reacted to what happened to me, because my adult family members did not live with us. It was just my mom, my sister and I.

I've always been a private person, and I think I got that trait from my mom. My sister is the same too, so once something happens to us, we keep quiet about it and sort it out among ourselves. Another reason we didn't tell anyone else what happened is that we thought, 'What is it going to change?' Nothing! We realized that the more we talked about it to other people, the more it was going to get out there and escalate, yet we wanted it to be as controllable as possible. So, we did what we could to protect my reputation and that of the entire family. I was just grateful that I hadn't been raped or worst still pregnant at 16 years old.

As much as we wanted to keep what happened a secret in my immediate family though, it didn't stay that way for long. Unknown to me, my aunt held a grudge against my mom and I. She felt insulted that she had taken me in, fed and clothed me and even saw me through secondary school, but I had repaid her by running away from her home. She hadn't asked me why I ran away, but I knew she was angry at me.

So one day, the cat was let out of the bag at a family meeting. We usually had meetings as a family in my late grandfather's house. It was a yearly occasion, and a time when everyone gathered to discuss and take stock of how everyone was faring in their families, jobs, businesses etc. It was a general meeting, and the usual issues were discussed but somehow, it came to the issue of me running away from my aunt's house. I didn't realize that many of my family members were curious to know what really happened, but we had denied them of the opportunity because of our decision to remain silent about it. So, as my other aunts castigated me for repaying the good that was done to me with evil. Soon, they became furious because neither my mom nor I responded. But, as they talked on and on, I got mad and finally stood up to explain what had happened. I said that I told only a few people about the matter because I didn't want to cause quarrels in the family, but as it was, they had given me no other choice. So, I told them everything that happened. I said that I had evidence of the love letters if they needed to see them.

By the time I was done, they were all quiet. Even my aunt didn't have a response to what I said. After I waited a while and no one said anything, I walked out of the meeting. That was the last day I saw many of those that were in that meeting. Their silence spoke a thousand words to me. It was clear they didn't know how to respond, because the abuser was one of their own. I'm just grateful that I had ran away when I did. If I hadn't, I would have had myself to blame. After that incident, I moved on with my life. I went to another school to do my A levels, and it was at the Muslim school I mentioned earlier. That year was an interesting one for me because I made many new friends and had a lot of new experiences. It was also an unforgettable year for me because it was the year my mom passed away.

My mom's death

I was supposed to go to college immediately I completed my A levels but all my plans changed with the death of my mom. She was my sole caregiver and sponsor of my education. She took care of my sister and I, so how was I going to cope without her? That was one time I really questioned the purpose of my life. Who was going to take on responsibility for me? I had a father who wasn't interested in me. My older siblings were all still struggling to find their way in life. My uncles and aunts all had their own families and responsibilities and didn't owe me anything.

To make matters worse, after my revelation at the family meeting, I found that many of my uncles and aunts did not want to associate with me. That attitude taught me a great lesson, because I wondered if they expected me to have stayed in that situation and get raped. I didn't know their perspectives, but I know I did what was right by me. I ran away to save my life.

My mom had complained of stomach trouble which only affected her for two days; the 23rd and 24th of December of that year. We called in a nurse to treat her, but on the 25th of December—Christmas day—she died. Her death affected my siblings and I, but it also opened my eyes to the world in so many ways. It made me see family members and friends for who they really are and made me get on my feet and take my wellbeing in my own hands. It made me stronger emotionally and psychologically and better equipped to make difficult decisions. It also made me more careful, intentional and strategic about my life. I understood that I had no one who could leave everything and come running to me if I got into any kind of trouble. That thought humbled me and made me mature and wiser than my years. For my sister on the other hand, my mom's death did the opposite. It made her lose interest in everything, and she became at a loss of how to carry on with life. She was closer to my mom than I, so it took a longer time for the vacuum left by my mom to be filled in her life.

While I resolved to look for a job or go somewhere else to work and move on with my life, my sister was willing to hold on to everything that was my mom's. This affected her mentally and for a long time, she didn't move on with her life.

As for my other siblings, my mom's death definitely brought us closer, because we had to mourn and talk about things that happened in the past, as well as plan for our future. On the part of my dad, after my mom died, I think he felt responsible for us and tried to get close to us and fill the vacuum my mom left behind, but it was rather late. We had all become adults who didn't need his fathering so much anymore. We were all old enough to make our decisions, do what is best for us and live our lives the way we deemed fit.

With these thoughts in mind, I set out to make meaning out of my life. I was determined to make my mom proud, because I knew the plans she had for me. I no longer had anyone to feed and clothe me, so the first thing I thought of doing was to get a job. I was 18 years old and old enough to work. I knew I might not find a professional job because I had only my O level results, but I was sure that I could find a paying job that would be enough for me to feed and clothe myself with. I also knew that I was going to have a long break from school before I went to university, and I hadn't even figured out how I was going to make that happen. I was also looking for ways to get busy, get over my mom's death and stay sane.

After a few weeks of applying, I got a job at one of my uncle's photo studio. He taught me how to take photographs and edit them professionally. I also worked as a receptionist at the studio and learned proper customer relations.

I had the opportunity to meet different kinds of clients and handle them professionally. That knowledge came in handy when I came into the public eye and had to relate with people from different walks of life. My uncle paid me a low salary, but I didn't mind; I had plans for the money. I saved a large part of it and processed my first international passport. I had plans to do a diploma course in journalism and immediately I completed it, I would travel to another country to find greener pastures. So. I worked for some months and saved up some more money, but it wasn't anywhere near what I needed to see myself through school. So, I had no choice but to look for a sponsor.

Armed with the little money I had saved up, I reached out to some of my rich uncles whom I knew had a lot of money. Some of them had even adopted children and sponsored them through schools, and I thought they would be able to sponsor me as well. So, after I got my A level results from the Muslim school, I went to them and explained my plight, but they turned their backs on me. It was the most painful thing for me at that time, and I would never forget it. What was more painful was the fact that I knew that they had the money and could help, but they decided not to. I was 18 years old and I was coming to my wit's end, but I was determined to go to university. I didn't run away from shame to continue my life in mediocrity. No! I deserved more and I was going to get it in every proper way possible.

Having looked through my extended family to see who could help sponsor me through university and found none, I turned to nonrelations. My mom, my sister and I had a small circle of neighbors and friends around us, so I began to think through that circle. I didn't know how it was going to happen, but one thing I was very sure of was the fact that I wanted to go to school and get an education.

I was sad that my mom died, but contrary to what people thought that it would take the drive to continue and be successful out of me; it did the opposite. It fueled my desire to succeed and make my mom proud. I knew that one thing she wanted for all her children was for us to be educated, successful and attain heights that she couldn't reach in her lifetime, so I decided early on that I was going to do just that. I wanted her to look down on me from heaven, smile and be proud of what I achieve in life.

Getting my diploma

With this decision in mind, I began to reach out to my mom's friends and other family members I knew. I went to see one of my maternal aunts who was friendly and kind to us when my mom was alive. I figured she could help, so I told her what I planned to do. I knew she didn't have a lot of money, but she had a very good job at that time. She was the one who sponsored one of my elder brothers through school, and I didn't want to be another burden for her. But I knew she understood the importance of education and if there was anyone who would go out of her way to put me in school, it was her. So, I tried my chances and went to see her. She asked me what I wanted to do but honestly at that time, I didn't know what. However, I thought that being on television, presenting talk shows or doing something similar would be nice, so I told her about the journalism course. If I could get a chance to do a diploma in journalism, it would prepare me to be a media person. I knew I loved to talk and be creative and I wanted to explore that part of me. She enrolled me into the School of Journalism, and I got my diploma. That was the beginning of my higher education, I remain grateful to that aunt of mine today because if it were not for her, I don't know what my life would look like today.

My experience at the School of Journalism was an interesting one, and it was what I expected. We had studios, and we were expected to perform a lot of activities. I was very active and loved to take part in every activity. We did music renditions, dance presentations and drama acting. We also did stage plays and they were my favorite, because they enabled me express myself in any character I was given to play. One thing I really enjoyed getting involved in at the school was the Miss and Mr. Competition that was held. It was the last year of my diploma, and I contested for it, Surprisingly I won the title, and I was crowned the Miss UMCAT School of Journalism and Mass Communication of that year. It was an amazing year for me, and

I enjoyed the experience. I executed some projects in the school as the crowned queen and influenced other activities there. I also made a lot of friends and till today, I know a lot of media people in Uganda who started out from that school; they have a high success rate.

CHAPTER 6
WANTING MORE

After I finished my diploma, I decided that I wanted to go abroad and that was what took me to the country I currently live in. Going there gave me a fresh start, and the opportunity to meet new people, make different decisions and start the next phase of my life. I definitely wasn't thinking about pageantry or modelling; I just wanted to be a successful, confident and comfortable woman. I had given up on it after trying my hand at some modelling stints, and they didn't work out. So, I thought perhaps it wasn't the career for me, and I started to do other things. I started a career in business and focused on it, but in 2018, I found a video of Miss Uganda on YouTube, and I liked it. I thought to myself, "Hmmm! This is nice", and that was it. My friends also saw it, and they thought it was a good pageant. Even though I never saw myself participating in my pageant, my friends had other ideas. They believed that I could do it and so they encouraged me. Way before we saw that video, they always thought I had a beauty queen hidden in me somewhere. I had gotten used to them saying things like, "You could be a beauty queen", "You're tall enough", "You're slim and elegant too", "You could be a successful model" and other variations of it. But, I usually said to them, "There's no way I can be a beauty queen", and we would laugh over it.

So, during the summer of 2019, I had booked my flight to go back home and I told my friends to expect me. They said, "Oh, perfect, this is good timing because auditions are going on for Miss Uganda, so you could take part in it." But, I said to them, "I don't have time for that; thank you so much." I thought that was the end of that discussion, but my friends would not hear it. They strongly believed that I was beauty queen material, so they said, "You know what? We will collect the forms and fill them on your behalf, and you will go to the auditions; agreed?" It was funny how tenacious they were, and thinking about it now, I'm grateful to have such friends in my life. They are friends who stick closer than sisters. They have been a worthy support system to me, because they believed in me even when I didn't see what they saw.

I agreed to their proposal to collect the forms, fill and submit on my behalf. They printed out some of my photos and attached them to the forms. They did practically everything for me, and we forgot about it. After sometime, I expected the pageant organizers to call me for shortlisting, but they did not. Maybe it was because I wasn't in the country, but I didn't receive any call or email, and I told my friends about it. They weren't deterred;

they told me I had to show up for the live auditions whether I was contacted or not. They had so much belief in me that it was humbling to see. So, I packed my bags and arrived in Uganda a day before the audition.

I got to the audition, and the whole place was filled with beautiful young ladies from all around Uganda and I thought to myself, "What am I doing here? This place is full of beauty." I almost went back home because I thought I didn't stand a chance where all these beautiful ladies were, but a voice said to me, "Stay, you're already here, you might as well make the best of it." So, I stayed. The auditions started and groups of three or four ladies were called in for each session. I sat patiently waiting my turn and just observing all that was going on. Then, late in the afternoon, almost all the ladies had been called in, but my name wasn't called. That was when I began to wonder what was going on. When one of the women ushering the ladies into the audition saw that I and few other ladies were still waiting, she came to me and asked, "Did we call you for the auditions?" That was a defining moment for me because I could have lied and said they did, so I could go in to be auditioned. But, I stuck with my principles of honesty and being a person of integrity and said, "No, I didn't receive any call."

"So, what are you doing here?" She asked again.

"I'm here because I applied," I said to her.

At that point, I had started to feel uncomfortable and ask myself again, "Oliver, what are you doing here? These people didn't call you for the auditions, you shouldn't be here. You shouldn't gatecrash this way."

Meanwhile, the lady continued to ask me questions, and the conversation had degenerated into a mild argument. While we were at it, one of the judges stepped out of the audition room and asked, "What is going on?"

The woman who had been questioning me, said to her, "There is this girl here, we didn't call her for the auditions, but she's here."

Before she had even finished speaking, the judge responded, "Yeah, let her in, let her audition."

To say I was stunned would be an understatement. My jaw dropped, because I certainly didn't expect that I would be allowed in to audition that easily, after the interrogation I had just gone through. The judge had looked at me and said, "She's definitely Miss Uganda material." I remember bursting into a wide smile and that gave me a lot of confidence to face the panel of judges. I thought to myself, "At this stage, I know I can do this." So, I changed into my audition clothes; a bikini, and went in with the last group of girls. We had waited all day, but I was grateful that my wait wasn't in vain.

At the audition, I was nervous and I remember telling the judges that I was nervous. But, they laughed and encouraged me to be confident. From that audition, I got into the next round and became one of the contestants of the Miss Uganda 2019 Beauty Pageant.

We took part in different challenges like sports, runway catwalks and talent shows. It was mandatory to participate in the talent shows but because I knew that I didn't really have any talent to showcase, I chose to exhibit my skills as a journalist. So, I anchored news as a newscaster and got one other girl who also claimed not to have any talent to do the reporting. Both of us worked together, and it was a beautiful presentation. We also had sporting activities and that was one area I had high hopes on because I am very good at sports. I put in my best but someone else won the title. On the whole, I had a lot of fun but honestly speaking, I hadn't seen myself getting that far in the pageant bootcamp. It was something I didn't prepare for, but by just being myself I stood out and aced a lot of the activities. For me, it wasn't like a competition so that made me feel at home. I felt like I was on a summer holiday, and I planned to enjoy myself and make a lot of new friends. So, I looked out for the contestants and helped them give their best at any task they were given to do. I was also a good team player, and I think that went a long way in helping the judges make the decision to crown me as Miss Uganda 2019.

Another factor that worked in my favor was the fact that while we were at the bootcamp, the girls voted me as Miss Congeniality. It came as a surprise to me, because I knew there were other amazing ladies there who could have been voted as Miss Congeniality. So, I got curious and asked some of the ladies why they voted for me. Many of them said I was approachable, friendly and easy to talk to. One of them said I was easily the best person to run to if she had a headache, because I would look for Panadol for her. I didn't know that all those titles were going to surface and that my attributes would count. I was just being my authentic self and doing things that I would have done for anyone anywhere else. Twenty-two of us made it to the presentation night, and I was contestant 22.

After I got the Miss Congeniality title while we were in the camp, we got ready for the beauty pageant proper and found out that the reigning Miss World was going to be in attendance. That held a lot of significance for me because I became the first ever Miss Uganda to be crowned by Miss World. She had flown into Uganda some days before, and we had done some charity work with her, but I didn't know that she was actually going to crown me. It all happened like a dream, and I kept pinching myself to see if I would wake up from it. This was something that my friends had seen me do even when I failed to see it. I felt so grateful to them for motivating and encouraging me, especially when I almost backed out.

The night of the crowning was beautiful, especially because my dad came to support me. It is something that I really appreciated and didn't take for granted, because he had a demanding job and had to really make out time to attend. I remember that I had called him days before and asked that he attend the pageant. He had responded that he didn't know what time he was going to be in town (he worked in another city) but if he could make it, he'd be there. And, he made it. The amazing thing is that he came straight to the pageant in his work clothes, because he didn't want to risk missing any part of the pageant if he went home to change into a ceremonial outfit first. It was nice to have that kind of support from him, and I'm grateful for it. Everyone deserves to have that kind of love from their parents.

Becoming Miss Uganda 2019

Becoming Miss Uganda 2019 came with a lot of benefits. First of all, I got to work closely with other NGOs and advocate for causes that I believed in. I desired to advocate for age-appropriate sexuality education for teenage girls and young women, and I had my reasons. I didn't just want to do it because I needed to have a cause to advocate for, as Miss Uganda. It was something I was passionate about because of the experiences I had gone through. Apart from my experience of sexual harassment, what I saw when I returned to Uganda after spending a few years overseas, made me quite sad.

After I completed my diploma in journalism, I moved to the Middle East and worked there for two years. When I traveled back home and around the time I began to prepare to be a part of the Miss Uganda beauty pageant, I saw some of my friends. Many of them were either married, had become single moms or were pregnant with no one to take responsibility. They were teenagers or in their early twenties, and I was devastated by it. They didn't have an education, a job or a trade. They were just at the mercy of the men who impregnated them. I knew immediately that it was a cause I wanted to get involved in and talk about. We needed to find a solution to it, and I was prepared to use my platform as the reigning beauty queen of Uganda to do that. I could relate with what the girls had gone through or were going through and was aware that I could have been a part of the statistics if I hadn't escaped. The first thing my team and I did was to research why teenage pregnancy had become so rampart. Part of our discovery was the fact that sexuality education is lacking in Uganda and the entire Africa, because parents don't want to talk about it. Sex is an abominable thing to talk about in many homes, but the reality is that once a child grows into adulthood, his or her body will begin to experience sexual urges. It is a natural occurrence that cannot be ignored. It is therefore important to teach pre-teens, teenagers and young adults the A, B and C of sexuality education. They help to prevent sexually transmitted diseases and infections, as well as unwanted pregnancies. A stands for Abstinence. Abstinence means staying away from sex and practicing celibacy until marriage or until the time is right to be involved with a partner. B stands for Be mutually faithful. Mutual faithfulness is important for partners who are sexually involved with each other. It ensures that no partner brings in an STD, STI or HIV/AIDS from another person to infect the partner. C stands for Condom use. The proper and correct use of condom helps to prevent unwanted pregnancy, HIV/AIDS, STDs and STIs.

I saw the need to get the knowledge of these things to the populace, otherwise the rates of teenage pregnancies, STDs, STIs and HIV/AIDS would continue to be on the increase. I also saw the need to advocate for proper basic education for the girl child. I knew that if the girl child is motivated and empowered enough to remain in school, teenage pregnancies would greatly reduce.

Thus, we termed the two causes, Stop Teenage Pregnancy campaign and Keep-a-Girlchild-in-School campaign, and we began to create awareness and sensitize people about both projects. Initially, it was a tough cause to campaign for because it meant a lot of dynamics surrounding the girl child would change, but with time it was accepted. The African society being a patriarchal one didn't really give the girl child room to speak and be seen in society. She was expected to be silent and subservient to the male folks, but with the enlightenment and conversations that we started, I'm proud to say that the narrative is changing and the girl child is becoming more empowered.

The experiences I garnered by living abroad gave me boldness and courage to champion the causes I am so passionate about. I had seen firsthand what it meant for women to be emancipated and empowered to become all they could possibly be. I had seen highflying women and women in positions of leadership. I had come across women who dared many odds, to scale heights and achieve seemingly insurmountable goals. In fact, I am also a case in point. I looked at myself and thought that if I could do all I had done and made something amazing out of my life, any girl could do the same.

During my reign as Miss Uganda 2019, I thought it would be all glitter and glamor all the time but unfortunately it wasn't. Wearing the crown of Miss Uganda meant that I actually had to buckle down and work with NGOs and charities to meet the needs of my people. It meant that many times I had to get my hands dirty and do the physical work of ensuring that people were given what they needed and life was made better for them. I didn't have any problems with that because I loved to give back to society, but it was back-breaking and very demanding work. I remember that every time I traveled home from Dubai, I would pack two big bags of items that I wanted to give away. I love giving to people and putting smiles on their faces, so I was always on the lookout for opportunities to do it. Charity has always been a part of my life.

As much as I loved being my country's beauty queen, I wished that I didn't have to do so many TV appearances and interviews. I am a very private person and always likes to keep my circle small and intimate, but being Miss Uganda took that way from me, so I had to strike a balance. Sometimes, I would grant interviews all day and on other days, I would be in the eye of the paparazzi all evening. I certainly didn't like the invasion of my privacy, but there was nothing I could do about it. I had become a public figure, and people expected to have access to me.

However, whenever I could, I arranged for 'alone times' where I could just enjoy my own company. It is during those times that I regroup and have internal dialogues with myself on the next step to take. On the other hand, I enjoyed the fact that being Miss Uganda exposed me to so many important people in the country and in other countries. Right now I have connections, friendships and networks that I will always have access to because of my title as Miss Uganda.

Miss World 2019

Another highlight for me in my journey as Miss Uganda was when I took part in the Miss World competition. The competition took place in London and 120 countries of the world were represented. It was a huge privilege to have been there to represent my country and raise our national flag. At the pageant, I made a lot of friends whom I still keep in touch with and had an exciting time taking part in various activities. I won the title of Miss World Top Model and also became a Miss World cover girl on the Miss World magazine for that year. That was a blessing that I never saw coming because among all the 120 ladies, they chose my face and put it on the magazine. I also took part in the sporting activities and out of 120 ladies, I was one of the top 32 ladies and the best of all the 8 girls in my group in the sports category.

The Miss World Top Model title also exposed me to many modelling opportunities. Through it, I was able to participate in the New York Fashion Week and Fashion Week, Dubai as a model. There was also a head to head challenge where each contestant had to face another contestant head to head and talk about the projects they were working on back home. I spoke about the Stop Teenage Pregnancy and Keep-a-Girlchild-in-School campaigns and outlined the vision of the advocacy, the work we had done so far and the plans we had in future for girls and young women in Uganda. The audience, the people back home and social media were supposed to vote for the contestant who did the best presentation, and interestingly they voted for me. So, I won in that category as well.

Another beautiful thing for me at the Miss World competition was the connection that I made with other contestants. Those friendships have blossomed and grown over the years and in any country where those ladies are, I'm certain that I will be received warmly. Before I became Miss Uganda I had already traveled around a lot, but as Miss Uganda I didn't travel much. I spent most of my time in Uganda doing advocacy and executing other projects. So, when the Miss World season came, I had the chance to travel to the United States of America and take part in the New York Fashion Week. When I returned to Dubai; my second home, I got more congratulations from my university. There was media coverage from the university because they were proud that I won the crown as Miss Uganda and had gone on to represent my country at the Miss World beauty pageant. After that, I went to Jamaica on a personal vacation and met ministers of different ministries in Uganda. I also met some artists and other amazing personalities who I had great conversations with.

Becoming Miss Uganda 2019 reinforced in me the belief that being authentic pays both in the short and long run. I realize that once I made up my mind to be myself at the Miss Uganda pageant, it was easy for me to do things for myself and for others effortlessly. I also did not have any airs and that made me approachable by other people. These qualities made me emerge as Miss Uganda and opened doors for me to reach out to communities not only in my home state but country wide. It also gave me a platform to advocate for reforms that are in favor of the girl child and that will give her fair advantage and opportunities. My greatest joy is seeing that my advocacy eventually yields fruits such as raising funds for a girl who needs to go back to school and actually seeing to it that the girl is put in school and monitored till she graduates and makes something good of her life. That is my greatest achievement.

One other switch that I found to be tasking was having to switch from being Miss Uganda in my country and enjoying all the trips and perks that came with it, to going back to school in Dubai, becoming a student again and having to focus and concentrate on school work. It was hard while I did it but looking back now, I realize that it was a learning curve for me. It was also a beautiful experience, because it gave me a lot of exposure. People who heard about me and the work I was doing with the advocacy for girls and young women applauded it and showed a lot of respect for me; I'm grateful for that.

Living abroad

When I arrived in Dubai, I didn't know anyone, and I had nothing except my determination to succeed. So, the first thing I did was to get a job. I reasoned that if I had my own money, I could survive and start to put plans in place for my university education. In all I did, I didn't lose sight of the fact that I needed to get an education; it was my topmost priority. My first job was in real estate and because there were institutions where I could learn it, I enrolled in one of them and got the certificate to practice. Then, I got employment in a good company and gained relevant experience in two and a half years. Working in that company gave me the needed push to enroll in business school and get my university education. I found that business marketing suited me well and came naturally to me, and I knew instinctively that it was something I would excel at. Time has proved me right. I have closed more real estate deals than I can count, and I'm looking to venture into business as soon as all my plans fall in place. So, I'll say that moving to another country did me a lot of good. It opened up horizons for me and expanded my sphere of influence. It also made me more culturally accepting and versatile.

Meeting new people and making new friends helped me become more emotionally intelligent and grow intellectually. The stimulating conversations I have had in different situations over the years have made my world view evolve and become more robust. This place that I now call home groomed me in more ways than I ever thought it would, and I took those ideologies and perspectives back home during my reign as Miss Uganda 2019.

CHAPTER 7
YOU CAN DO IT TOO

The journey has not been an easy one, but it has definitely been rewarding. My team have successfully put some girls back in school. We also take into consideration the girls' preferences of the kind of empowerment they want. Some tell us expressly that they want to get an education, while others decide to learn vocational skills. With this in mind, the Miss Uganda team enrolls them in institutions that teach these skills. We realize that this is preferable by many girls than going to high school or university, because it saves time. So, they learn a skill, focus on it, graduate from the institution and start to work immediately.

With the Stop Teenage Pregnancy campaign, we have succeeded in changing girls' perceptions about sex. It is a primal need, but one that they have a control over. The first thing we do when working with these girls is to do a mind revamp and help them understand that they have much more in them, than just the ability to satisfy a man in bed and birth children. I believe that this teaching reached their hearts because when the COVID-19 lockdown happened, I was devastated because I knew it would be a tough period for many vulnerable girls. However, when I saw the numbers of girls that didn't get pregnant during the lockdown, I was glad. I know that the numbers of unwanted pregnancies rose in other areas during that period, but it was significantly lower in the areas we had campaigned aggressively in. It was a good sign that girls were listening to our 'gospel' and efforts to stop teenage pregnancy and taking appropriate actions.

The successes we recorded over time motivated me to go ahead and launch my foundation, The Oliver Nakakande foundation in February of 2022. One of the aims of the foundation was to identify the causes of the rising incidences of girls dropping out of school and address the issues. The scope of the foundation also includes empowering teenage mothers who have dropped out of school, because I believe strongly in second chances. Getting teenage mothers to return to school is one of my driving forces, as now more than ever, Africa needs to come together to cultivate the power of education.

During the period after COVID-19, we registered over 500,000 cases of teenage pregnancies in just about one and a half years in Uganda only. Some of these girls got involved in sex because they had to survive somehow; by giving their bodies in exchange for money to feed. Many of them got pregnant and didn't like the situations they ended up in, but wished to go back to school, if they had a sponsor. So I believe that if we give a chance to these girls, take them to a technical school to acquire vocational skills or universities to give them formal education, it will go a long way to rehabilitate and equip them for a more meaningful future. For these girls, education and enlightenment is the most powerful tool that can bring them out of mediocrity and poverty.

One of the ways my foundation ensures that girls who are already in school stay there, is by ensuring that the issues that cause them to stay away from school are addressed. For instance, every month, there are girls who stay away from school for days due to their menstrual period. They cannot afford to buy sanitary pads and tampons to use during that time of the month. So, in order to avoid getting stained and embarrassments, they stay away from school. For girls in many developing countries, this is a big issue and it is why May 28th of every year is World Menstrual Hygiene Day. The theme for the year 2022 is 'Making Menstruation a Normal Fact of Life by 2030. The overarching goal is to build a world where no girl is held back from taking part in her life's activities because she menstruates. By providing sanitary pads for such girls in Uganda, my foundation helps to achieve that goal. Though the foundation is targeting girls in Uganda at the moment, we have plans to increase the scope of our operations and make it a continent-wide affair.

Apart from focusing on the health and development of the girl child, at The Oliver Nakakande Foundation, we also believe that it is important to keep girls in school, not just for their sakes but for the sake of their communities and countries. The fact is when girls stay in school, they are less likely to get infected with HIV, STDs and STIs because of the awareness they will get about these issues at school. They are also less likely to have unwanted teenage pregnancies because they understand the implications of unprotected sex, become enlightened about the impact of education and are often too busy with school work to be carried away by the attention of boys or men. I also believe that education helps girls cultivate a healthy environment where they can create job opportunities from the skills they learn. This is in line with the global notion that when you educate a girl, you change the world. With these vision, the foundation seeks to cultivate the power of education in raising a generation of female leaders.

Another project I got involved in when I was crowned Miss Uganda 2019, was the Clean Water project. I worked with Ugandans in the diaspora under the umbrella of Ugandans in North America Association - Causes (UNAA-Causes), and I was the Clean Water ambassador. The project involved doing an inspection of areas where people don't have access to clean water and providing it. Many people in Uganda didn't have access to safe water and good sanitation, so we inspected such areas and provided solutions to the problems we found there.

That project went a long way to solve the problems of diseases like cholera that ravaged many communities in Uganda.

A word for every young person

One thing I know is that where there is a will, there is always a way. Sometimes, you may find that you have hit a brick wall, and you do not see any kind of light anywhere. Some days might be good, and some days might be bad; in fact sometimes, a whole period might be good, and a whole period might be bad. But, in the midst of all the bad days and bad periods, there is always hope for you as long as you have life. As long as you have breath in your nostrils, it is not over yet. What you need to do is develop a positive mindset. Believe that your dreams can come through, and they will. All you need to have all your needs met is inside you and that is your determination to succeed.

It is in times like that, that you need to think and ask yourself questions. Who can I reach out to, to help me solve this? Which friend, acquaintance or organization do I know? How can I solve this challenge? What do I need to do to get out of this problem? One thing I know for sure and have practiced over time is that the quality of friends you keep, determines how well your life turns out. Your network determines your net worth on so many levels: financially, materially and socially. This is why it is important to be intentional about the people you associate with. More importantly however is to be intentional about the vision you have for your life.

What are the short term and long term goals you've outlined for your life? This means what do you see yourself doing and achieving in the next three years (short term) and ten years (long term)?

Do you have a vision board? A vision board is a practical board that you can hang somewhere in your bedroom or living room and on which you display pictorial representations of your vision for your life. A vision board rides on the principle that as far as your eyes can see, that is what you will be empowered to accomplish.

Thus, as you see the pictures of the things you want for your life and the heights you want to be able to get to, everyday; your mental faculties and entire being will begin to align with getting you there. The universe also conspires to bring these things to reality for you as you see them every day and work towards their actualization.

Recently, I've been hearing a lot of suicidal cases. While I understand that people who suffer from depression up to the point of having suicidal thoughts have serious mental issues that need to be addressed by a professional psychologist, suicide is the way out. I can't tell you that I have always had everything rosy. From the experiences I shared in this book, it is clear that there were times I felt like life was not fair to me. I had barely been reunited with my mom after spending few agonizing years away from her, when she suddenly died. For a young girl, that was too much, but I resolved to move on with life. On some days when I find it hard to get out of bed and I'm tempted to stay there, I counsel myself saying, "Oliver if you stay here, nothing good and nothing new is going to happen to you. But, if you get up and go out and meet people, lot of good things will happen. You will learn new things, become a better person and move closer to achieving your life goals." That usually gets me moving in no time.

So, if you ever find yourself in such a situation, I'd like you to get inspired. There are many things you can do to take you out of that darkness and get you closer to your goal. Most importantly, you need to learn to plan ahead. If you reflect on my story, you will see that at every turning point, I had a plan. After I left home and went to live with my aunt, I discovered that life was not a rosy place. I found that many of the things I did at home and which my mom allowed, were not allowed with other people. That was when I began to learn how to make my own decisions and look out for myself. I made a plan to escape from sexual harassment and save myself from a precarious situation. I made a plan to leave my country and build a better life for myself after my mom's death. I made a plan to get into university and get an education. I made a plan to get into the Miss Uganda beauty pageant and make changes in the areas of society I am passionate about. I made a plan to work in real estate and build a career in it. I am a living example of how important it is to have a plan for one's life rather than wallowing in selfpity and wishing that a knight in shining armor will arrive to save the day. You are absolutely responsible for the outcome of your life.

I need you to understand that you are unique and special in your own way. there is no one like you in the whole wide world, and I do not say it to flatter you, I say it because it's the simple truth. God is very intentional when He creates us, He doesn't create any two human beings to be completely alike. That is why our fingerprints are different. In fact, the fingerprints of the most identical twins are different. That is how unique we all are. You should also understand that we all go through different paths in life, and it's ok not to have it all figured out. But, as you take small steps in the right direction, you will get to your destination, if you keep at it. Just be yourself. Keep doing the right things and focus on what really matters. Trust yourself, believe in yourself and accept yourself before you do it to others. That way, you will turn out a whole and confident human, and it's the only way to win the biggest fight of your life—the one within. I'm rooting for your success.

ABOUT THE BOOK

Have you ever felt helpless or being in a situation where you didn't see a way out?
Have you ever felt the odds stacked so high against you that you gave up all hope?

Has it ever felt that life is unfair to you at every turn?

If you answered 'yes' to any of these questions, this book was written with you in mind. In it, Oliver Nakakande, exMiss Uganda 2019 bares it all and shares her story of struggle to be the woman she is today. She shares how she faced unpleasant and hopeless circumstances as a young girl living in Uganda, and how with sheer grit and determination, she turned things around for her own good.

In The Escape; How I Ran from Shame to Fame, she gives an exposition of how she fought and escaped sexual abuse and a life of potential shame and mediocrity, to a life of fame and fortune. If you desire to learn how she did these and want to be inspired to become a better version of yourself as a girl or woman, flip to the beginning to start.

ABOUT THE AUTHOR

Oliver Nakakande is an international humanitarian, fashion model, and speaker who won the Miss Uganda title from 2019 to 2021. She was born in Kampala, Uganda.

Oliver had a tough childhood after she lost her mother at 18 years old, but while living with relatives, she was allowed to pursue her education; where she excelled. This period is best explained in Oliver's words: "When you have nothing, and you know that there's no one to pick you up if you fall; you know you must stand. This is why I resolved early to work hard to succeed". Oliver's determination led to her proudly bagging a Diploma in Journalism from the prestigious School of Journalism, UMCAT in Kampala, Uganda. She is currently studying Marketing at Middlesex University in Dubai, United Arab Emirates.

After relocating to the United Arab Emirates, where she also went into modeling, Oliver joined the Dubai Real Estate market as a real estate professional. While at Middlesex University, she participated actively in the university's basketball team and volunteered in various activities.

From a young age, Oliver has witnessed a lack of opportunities for girls and women in Uganda, and she promised herself that she would make a difference someday. That opportunity came when she applied to the Miss Uganda competition. Her main goal was to deal with the human rights issues affecting girls and to lend her voice to the UN Sustainable Development Goals of gender equality, quality education, good health and well-being, as well as clean water and sanitation.

As Miss Uganda, Oliver stood out at most competitions and events that she participated in. At the Miss World Pageant in London in 2019, she was the best in the head-tohead challenge Group 18, defeating representatives from Vietnam, Cambodia, Mauritius, and Laos. She was the first Miss Uganda to grace the cover of the Miss World 69th edition magazine, and she was the 4th runner-up in the Miss World Top Model 2019. Oliver is a lover of sports, and her abilities shone as she qualified as a finalist in the athletics division.

She is the first young black woman to compete in Miss Universe UAE.

As she traveled the world as Miss Uganda, she became an international model, participated in the New York Fashion Week and discovered a platform to share her passion for human rights.

Oliver is passionate about empowering teenage mothers who have dropped out of school and is an advocate for second chances. Encouraging teenage mothers

THE ESCAPE

86